Peggy Louise Parrish
Parma, Idaho
All Cover picture artwork and interior artwork by Peggy Louise Parrish
All Interior Text by Peggy Louise Parrish

ISBN -13: 978-15144265261

Printed in The United States of America

THE YOU'LL LIKE LETTER Y

Coloring Book

By Peggy Louise Parrish
C. 2017

Welcome to the letter Y. While there are not a lot of words that start with Y, many words end with Y. If you are making signs with names, you will often need a letter Y. Most of all the wonderful word YES and the words You, You'll, You're and You all will always start with letter Y.

These Y letters are just waiting for you to choose your choice of colors. The preferred medium for these pages is a quality set of colored pencils. However if you chose markers, ink gel pens, paints or watercolor pencils make sure you place a piece of scrap paper under your work. Feel free to make a few copies of the black and white color pages that you want to try in different color schemes. Remember to keep the artist initials PLP on the letter page and not to sell anything you try from this book.

If you enjoy this book try some of my other letter books.

Thanks for visiting this book with your colors.

Artist PLP

Peggy Louise Parrish

Letter Y is so pretty when it's colored

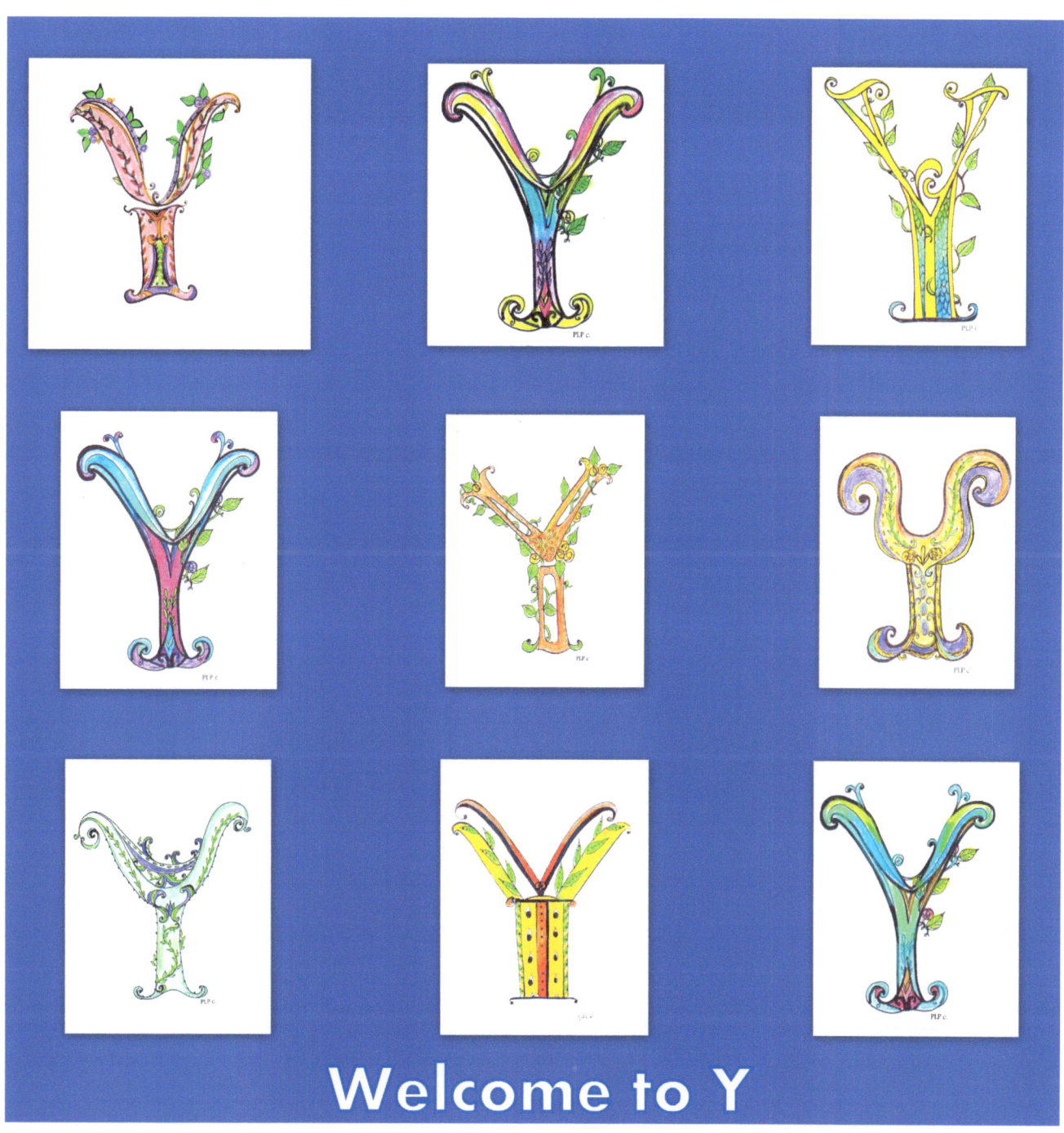

Welcome to Y

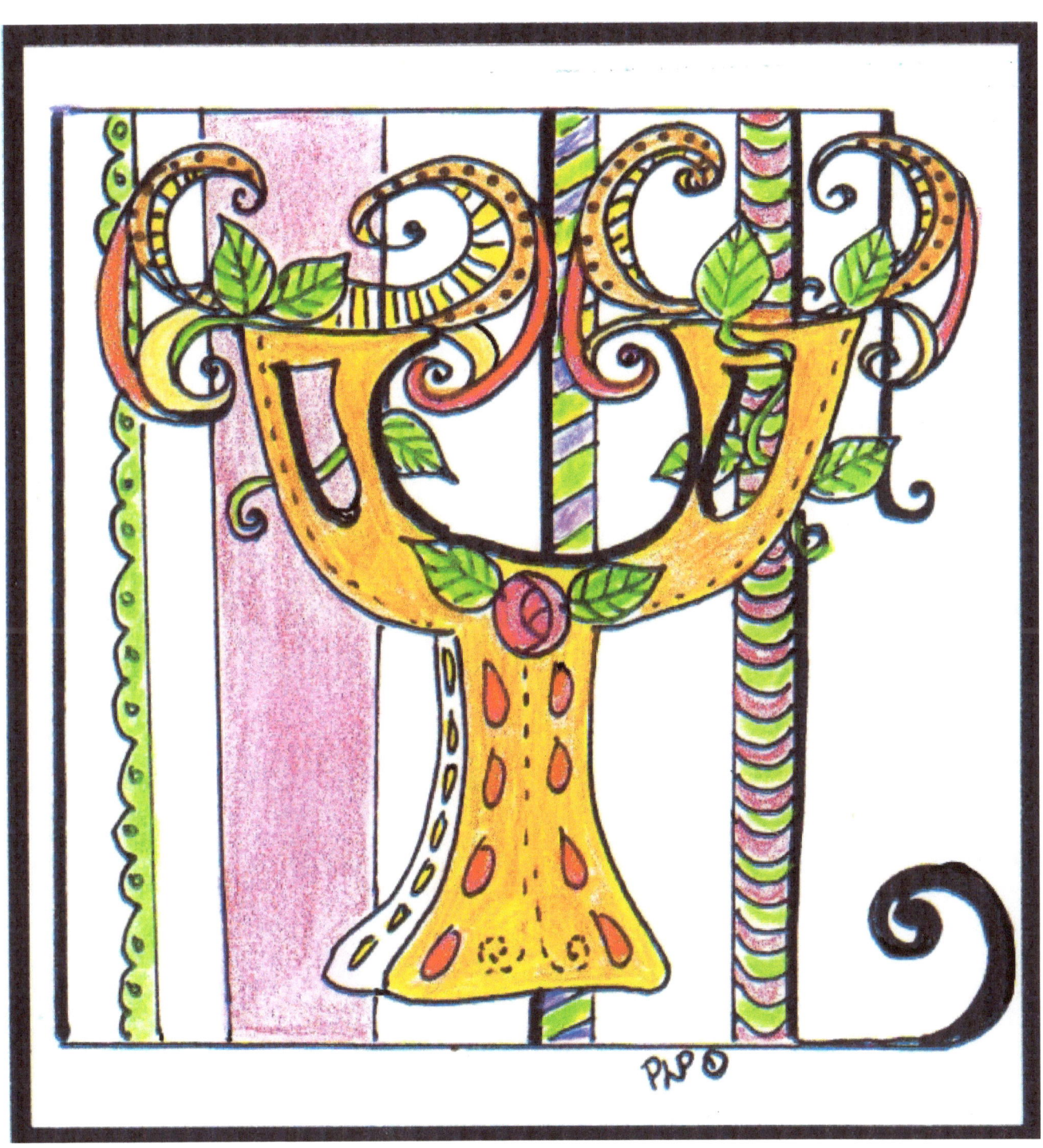

9

The Y letter can be lovely out in a rose garden

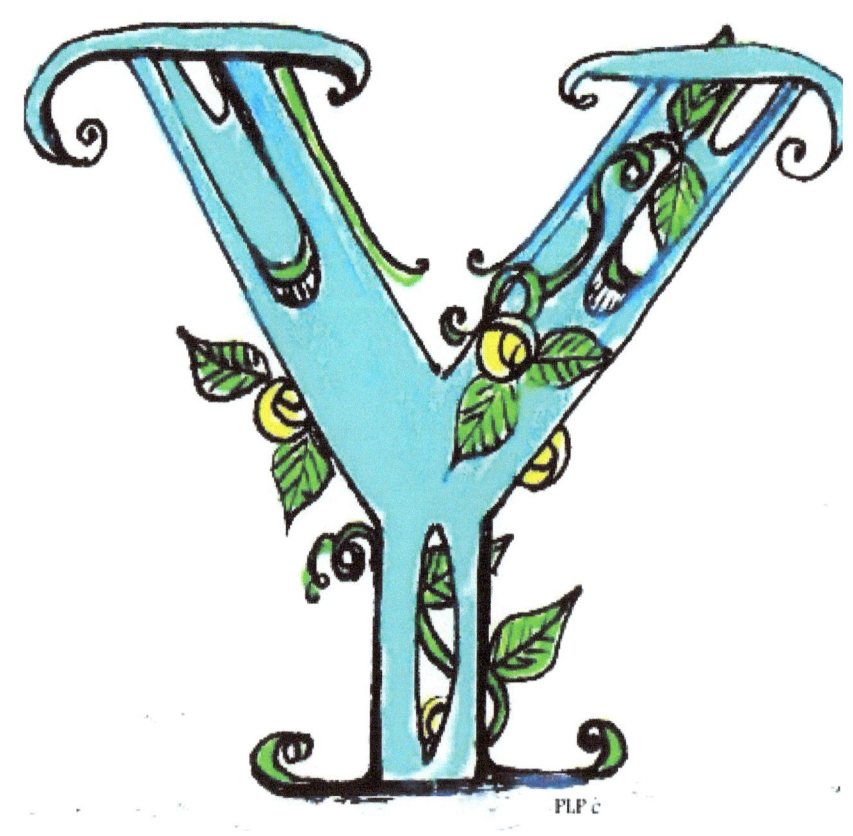

Letter Y can enjoy The Cowboy World

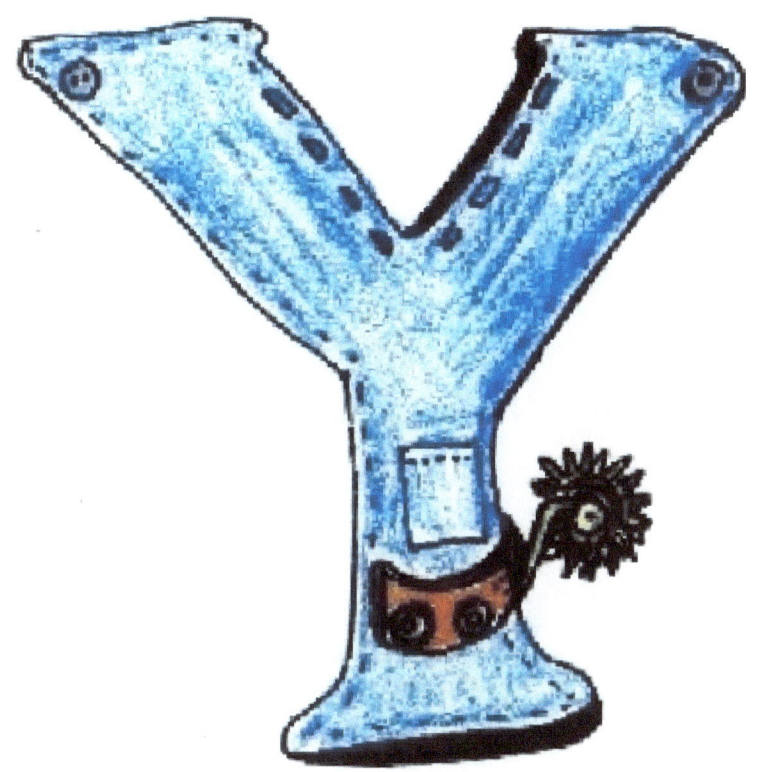

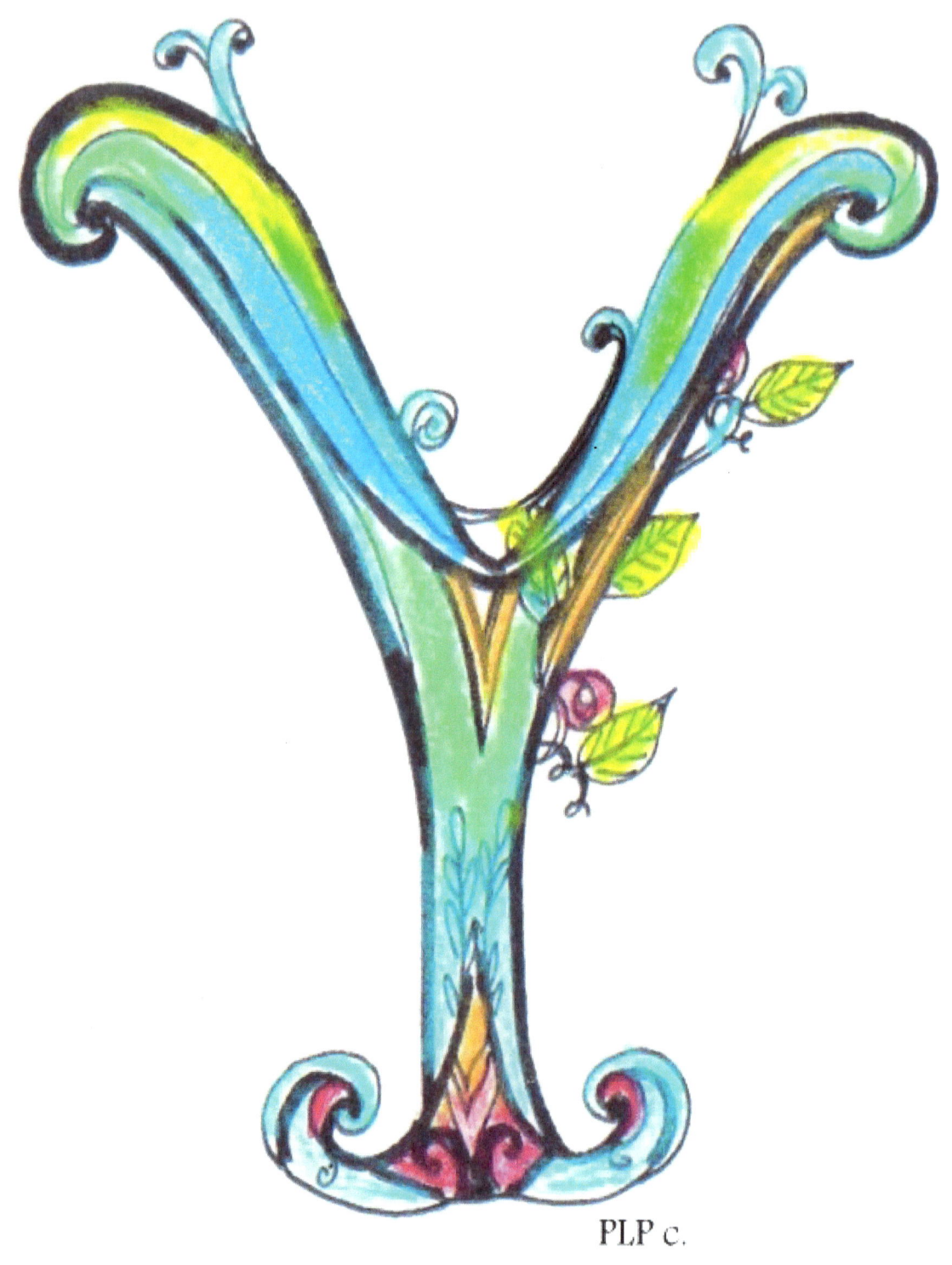

PLP c.

12

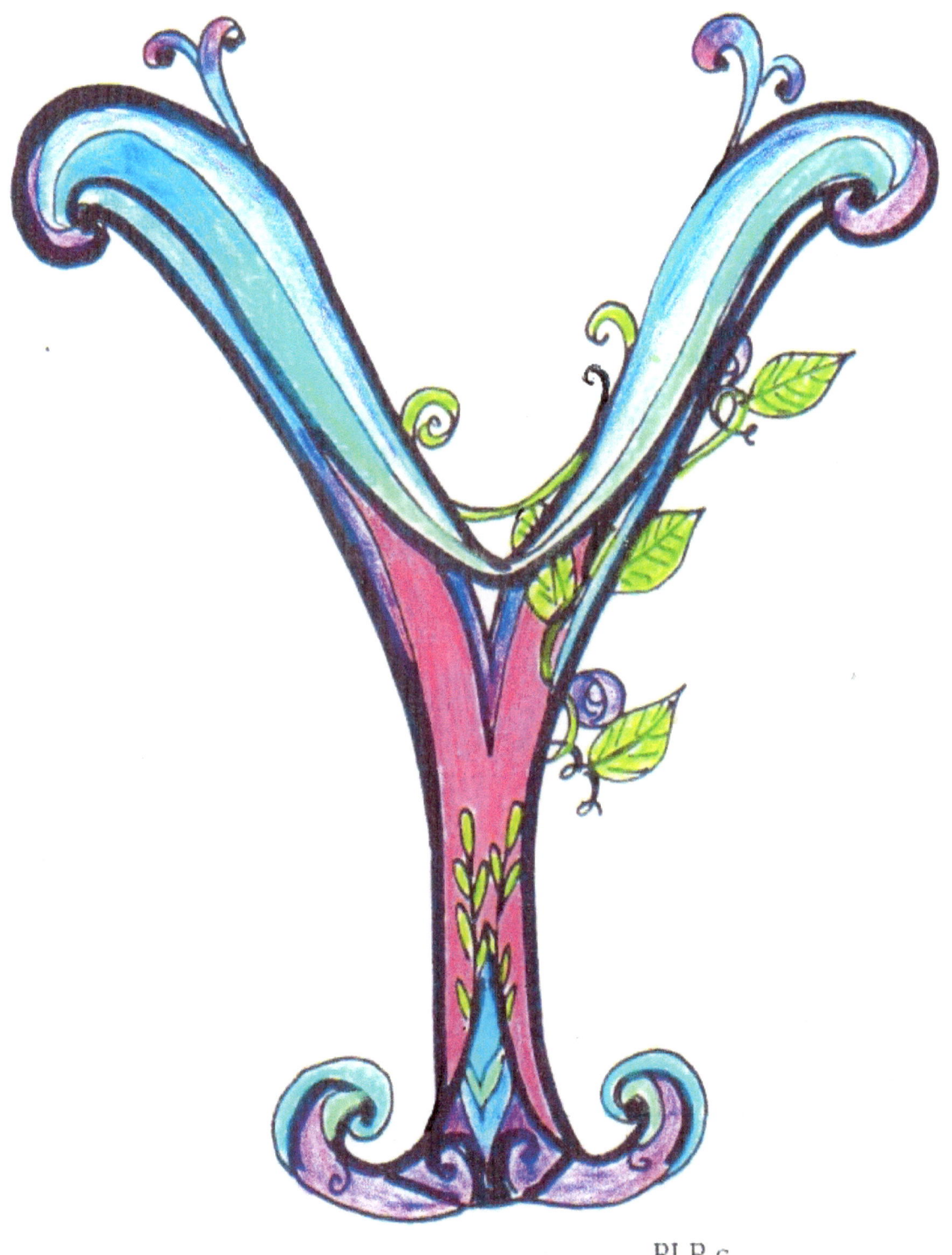

PLP c.

13

This is why YOU"LL like the Letter Y. It can be interesting to color, fun to decorate and always needed for words like YOU and YES.

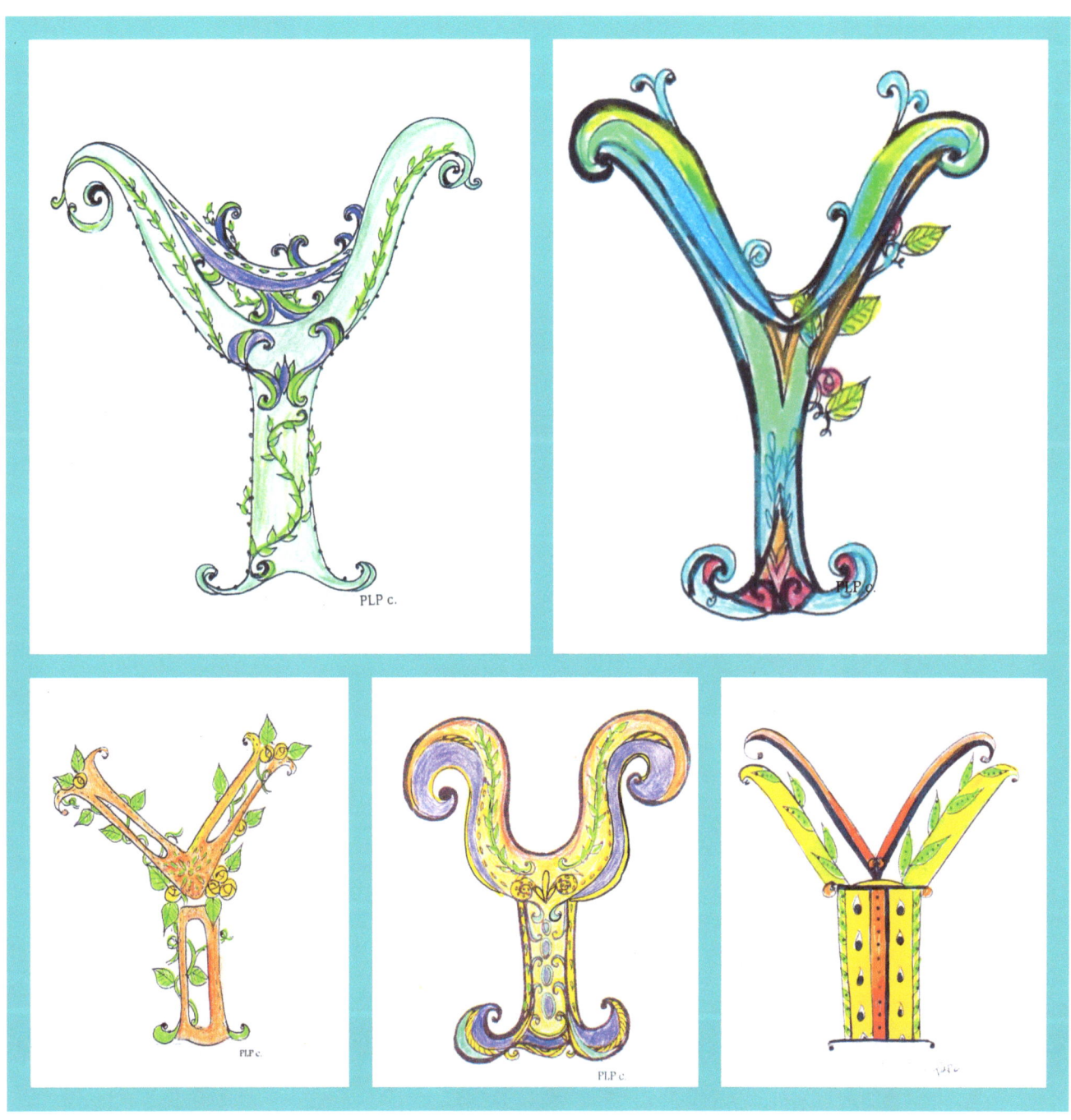

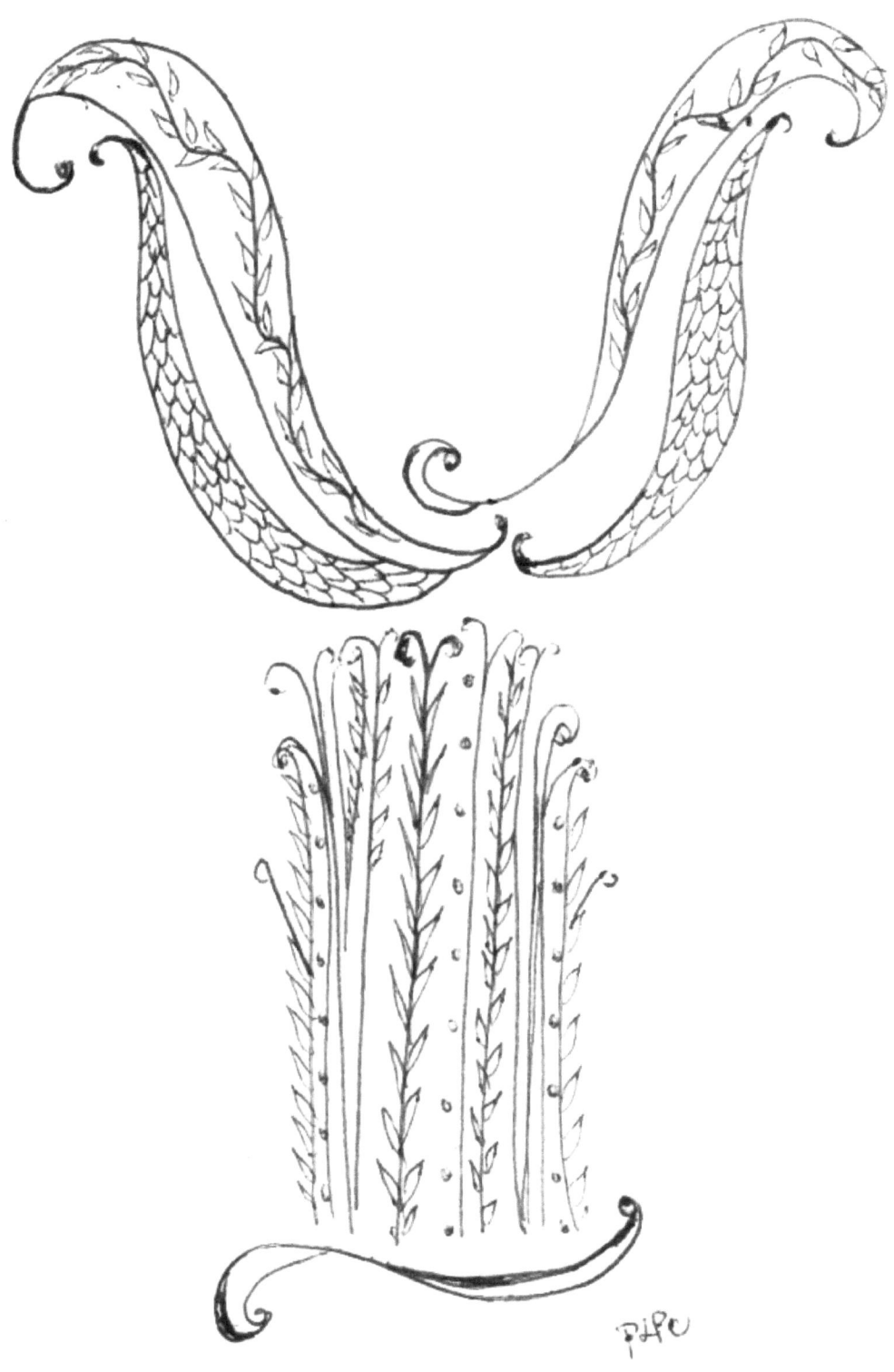

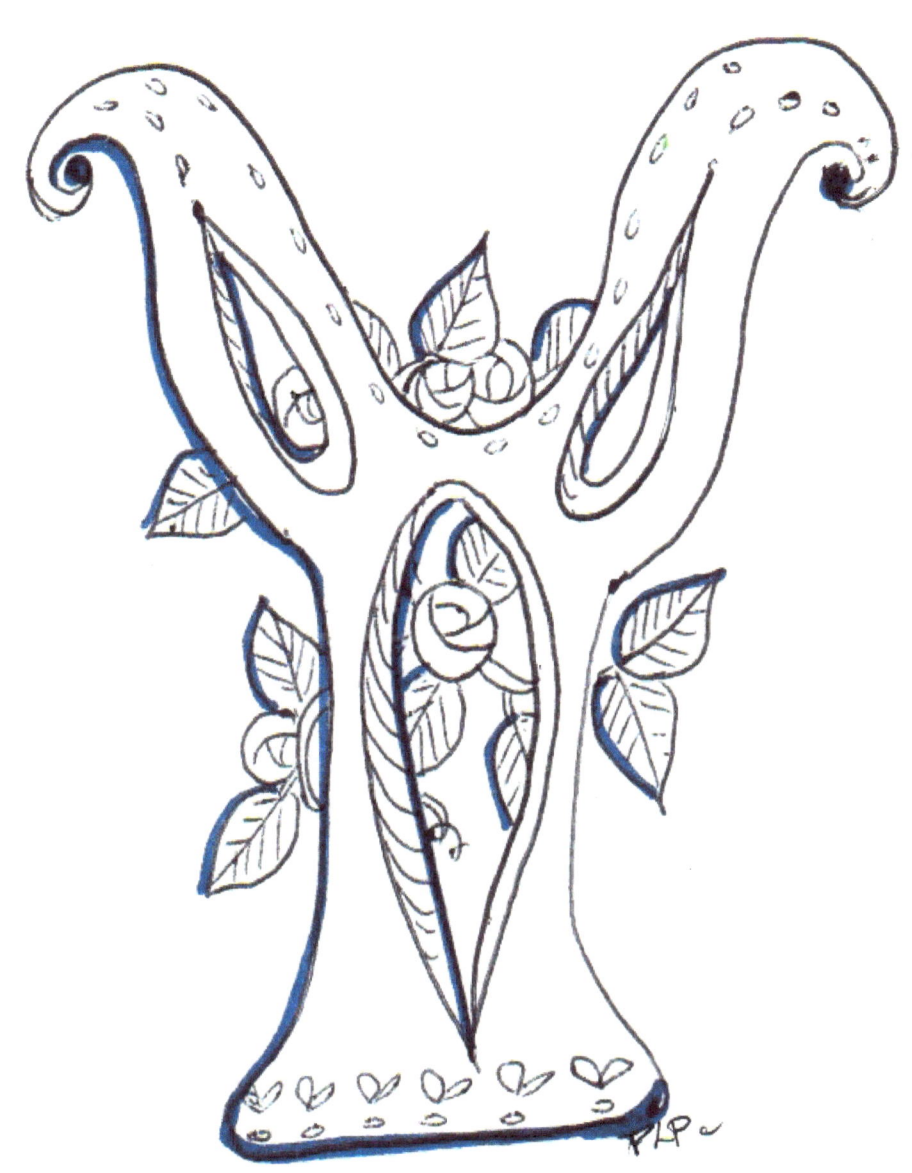

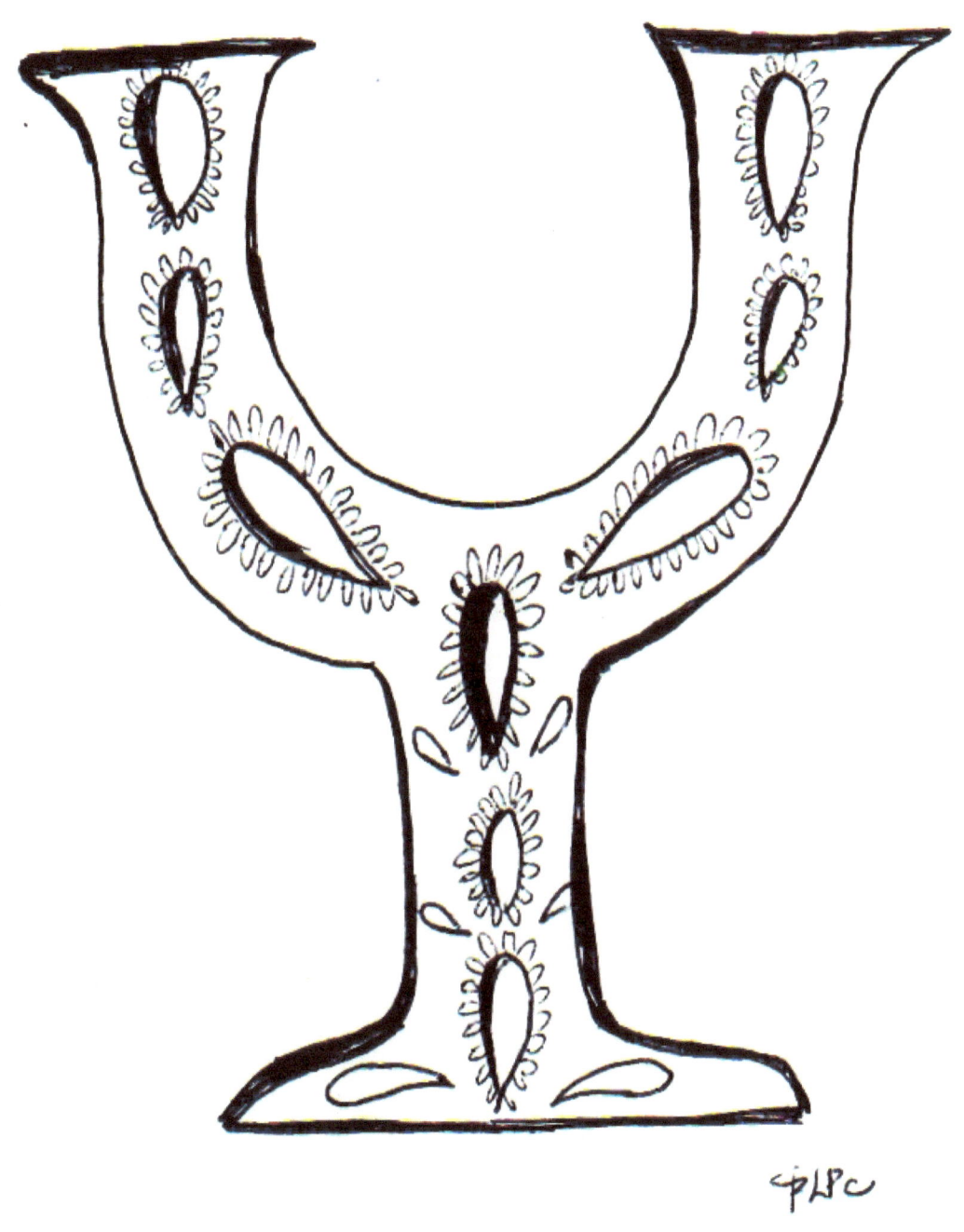

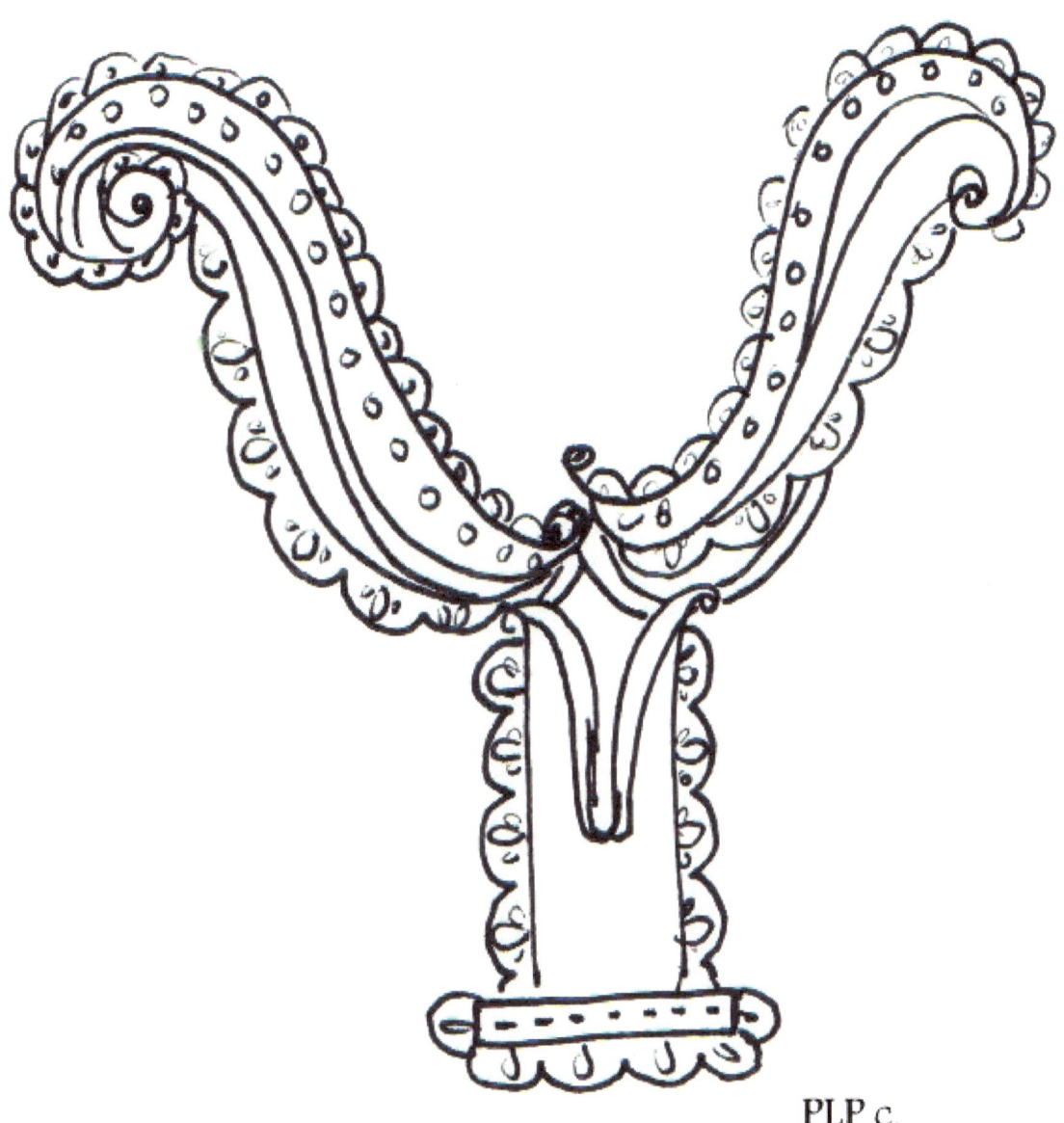

PLP c.

23

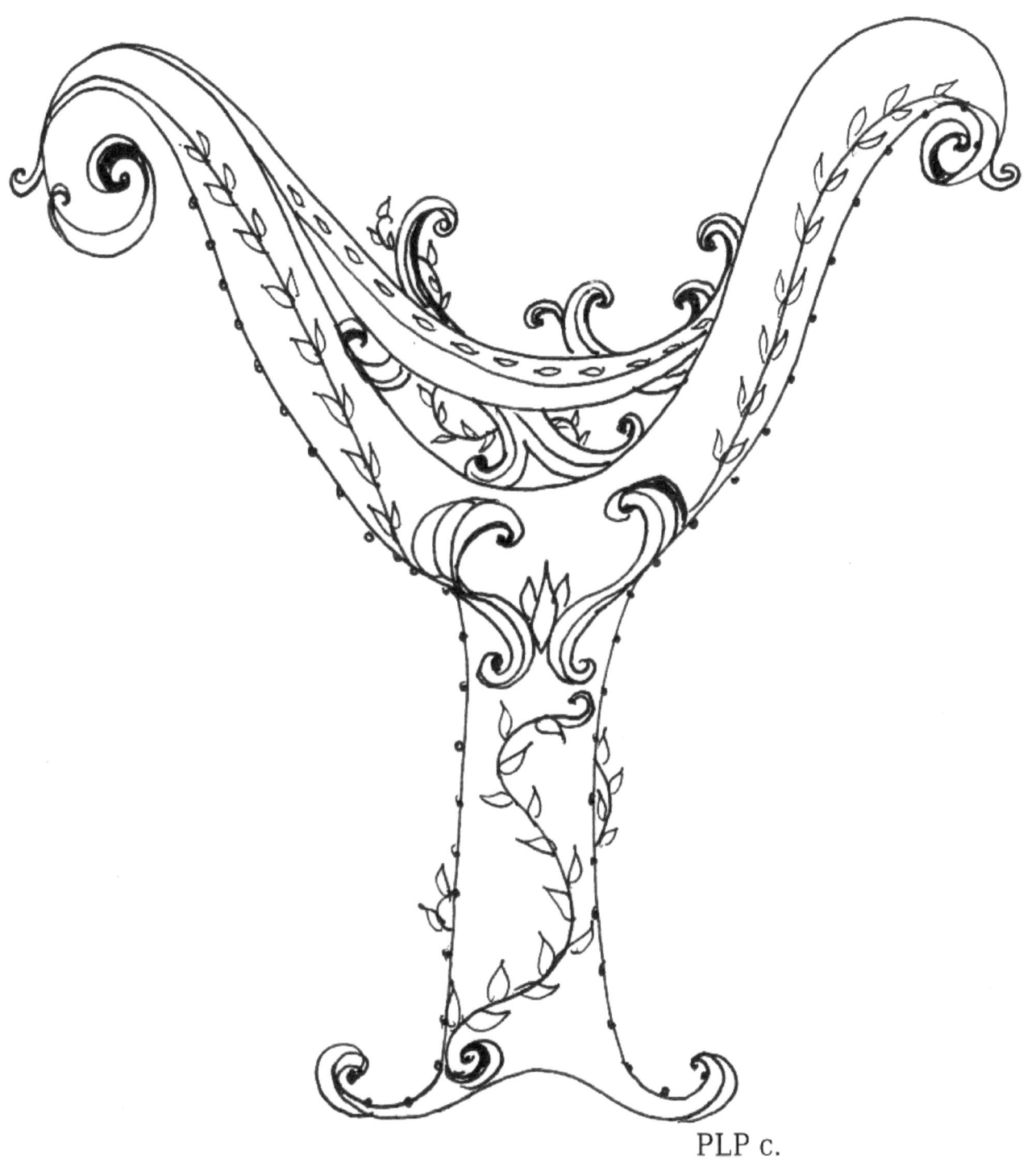

PLP c.

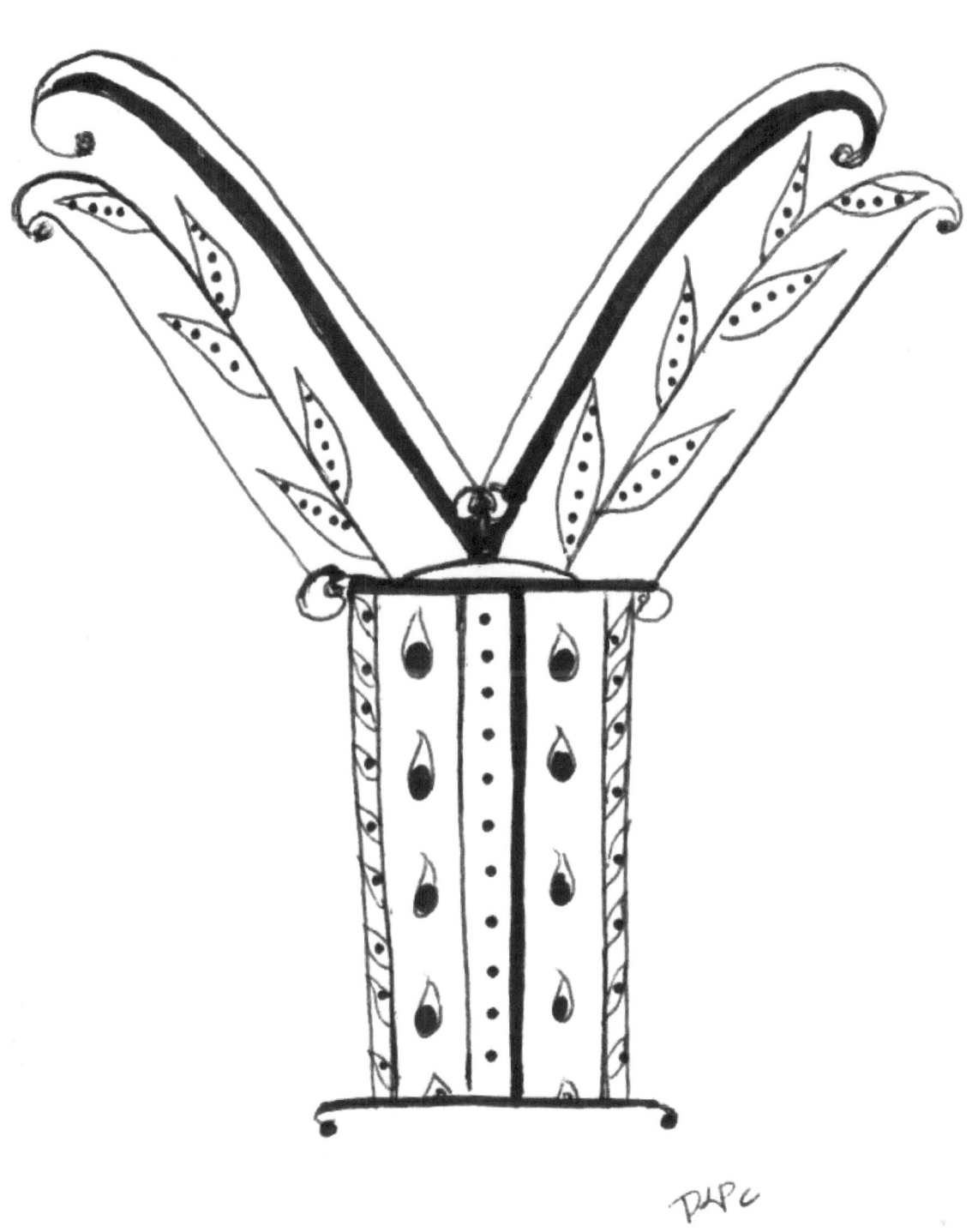

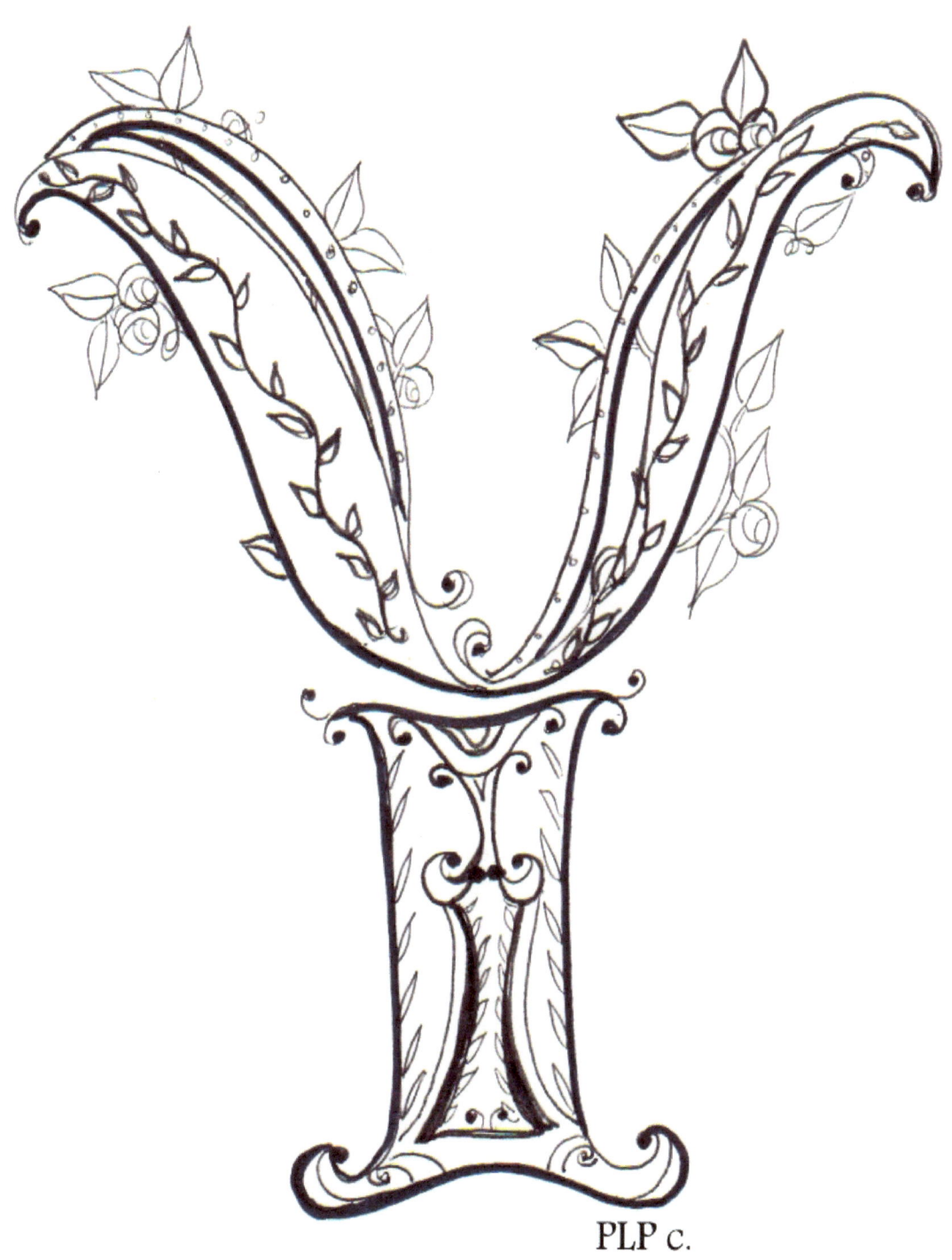

PLP c.

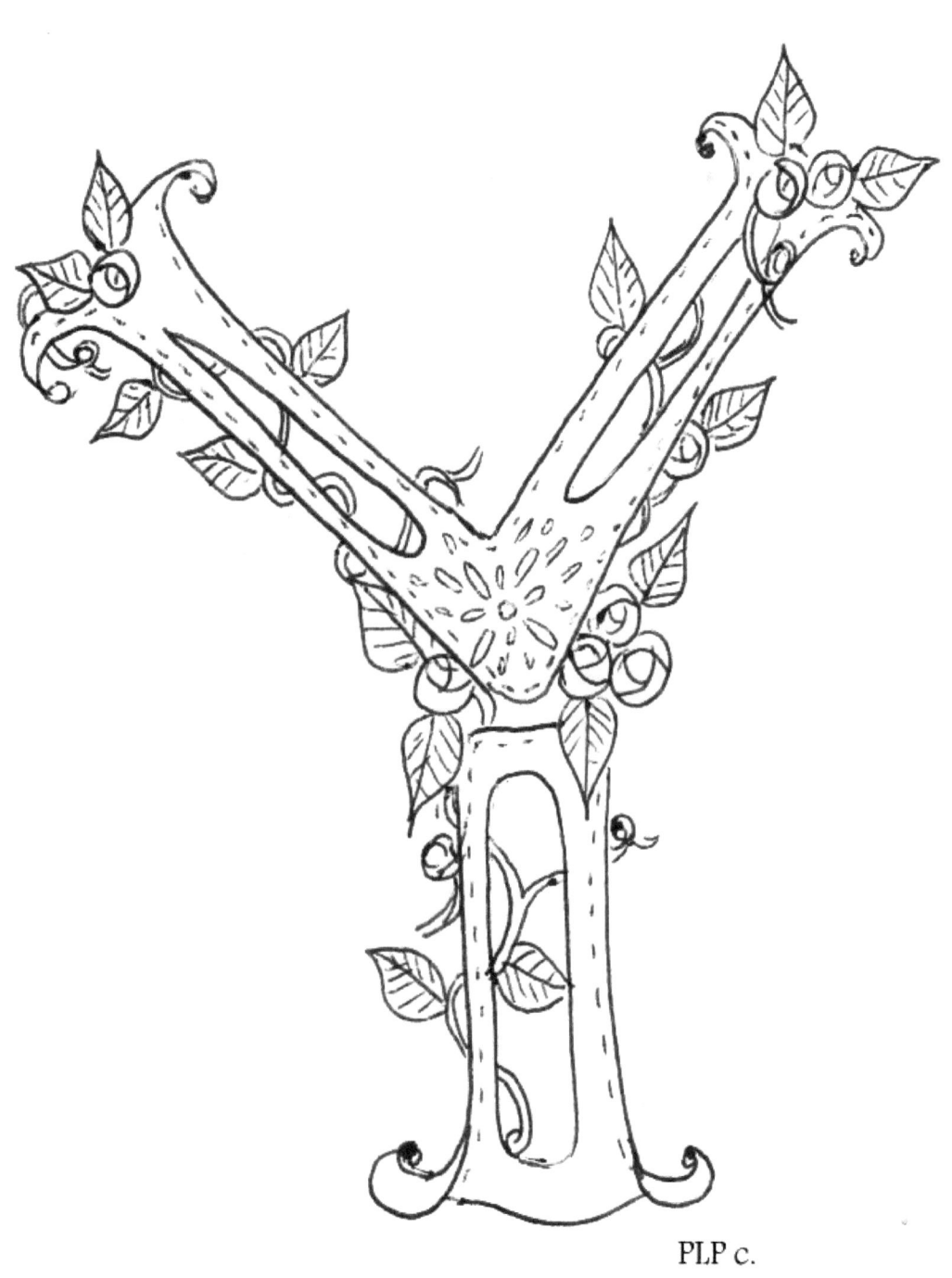

PLP c.

31

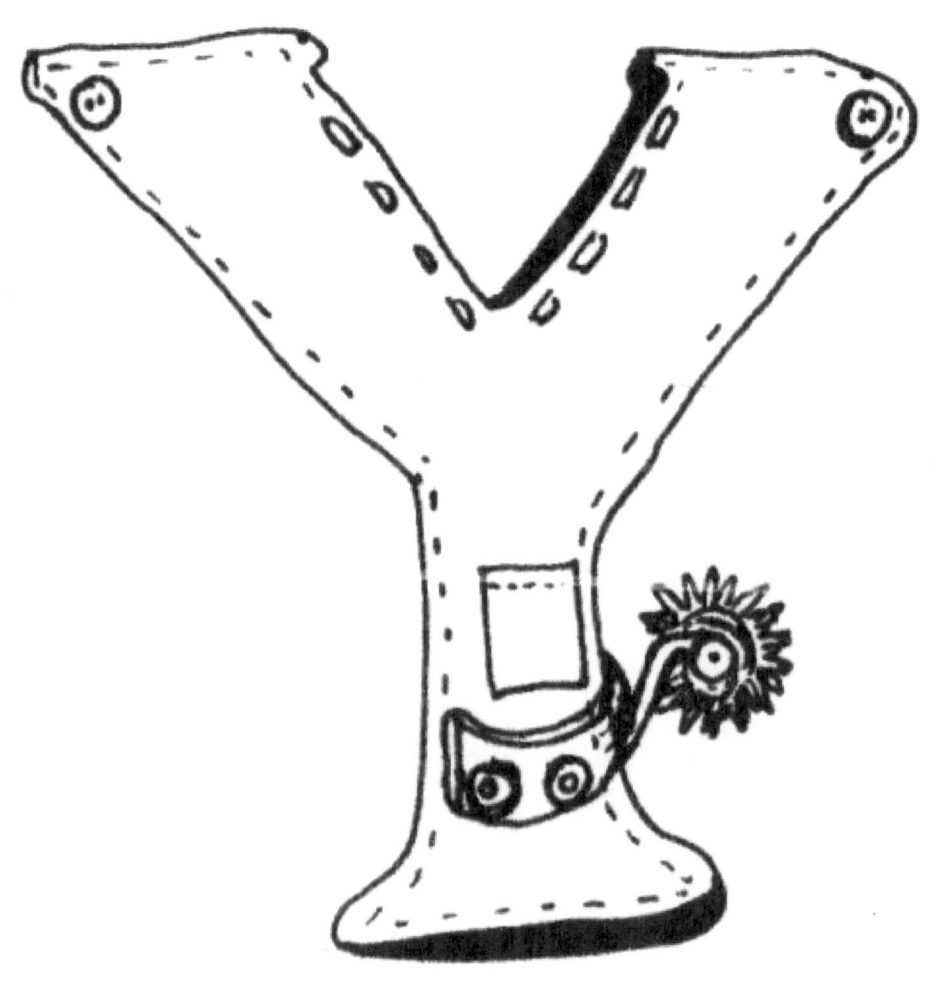

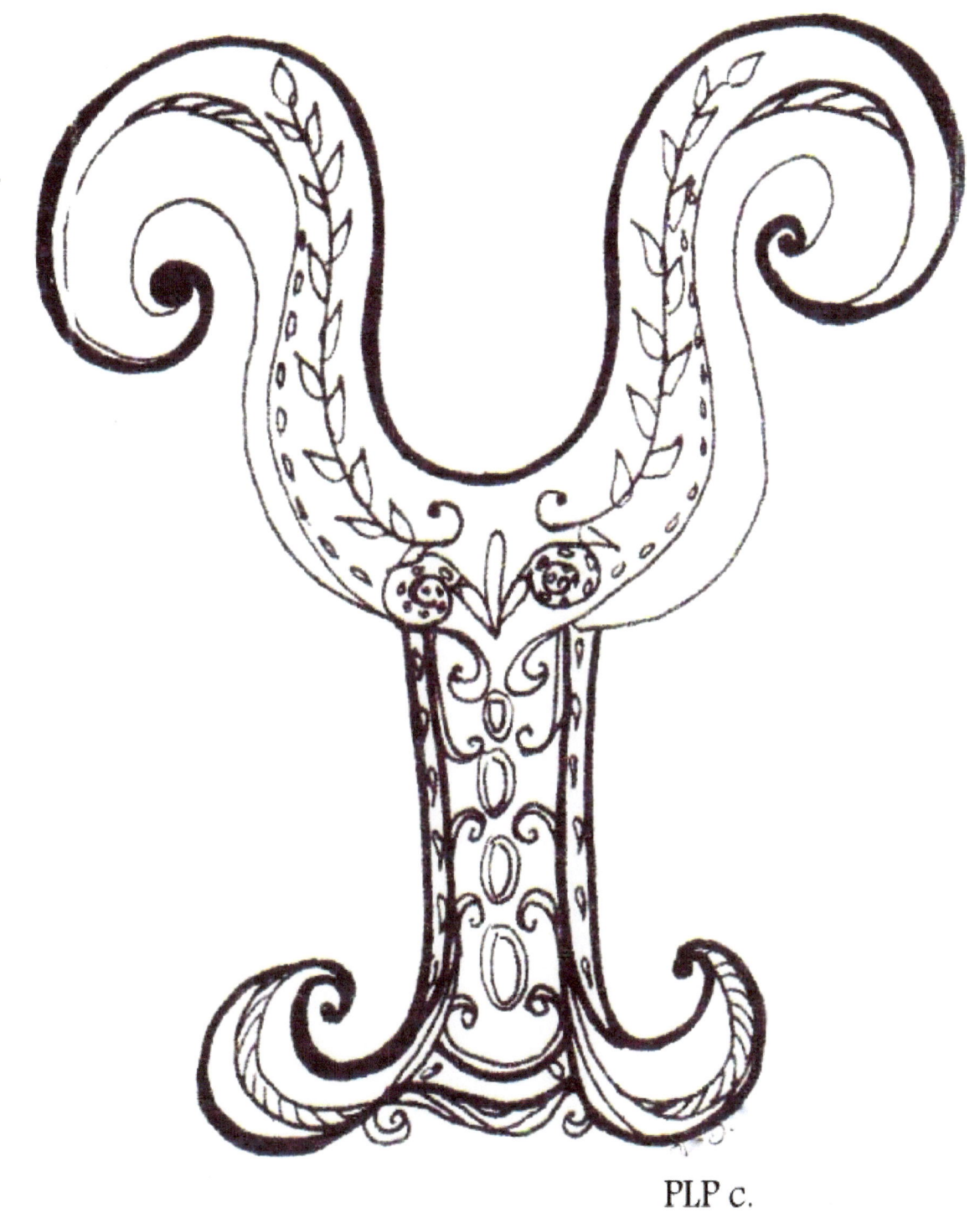

PLP c.

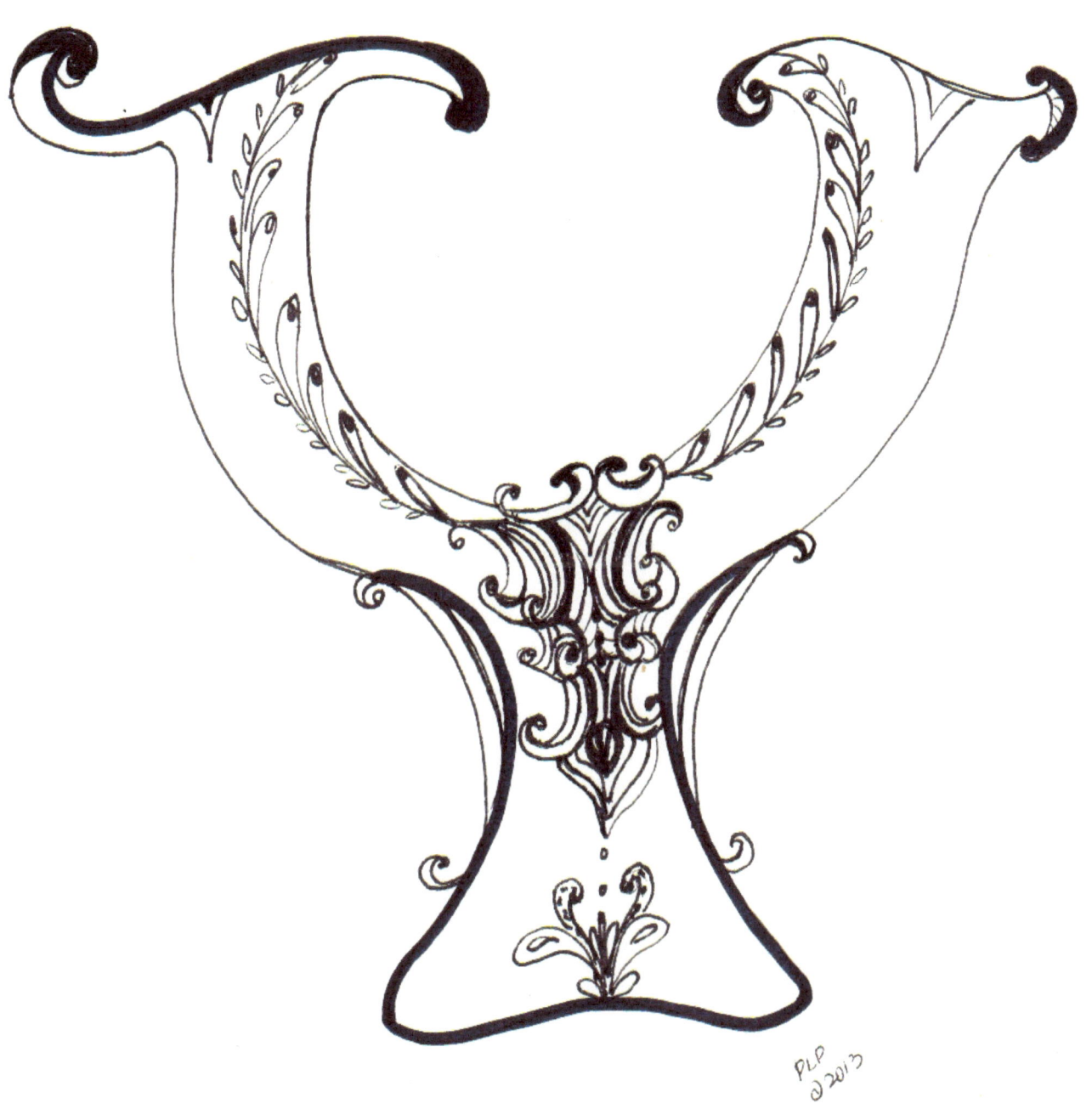

PLP
2 2013

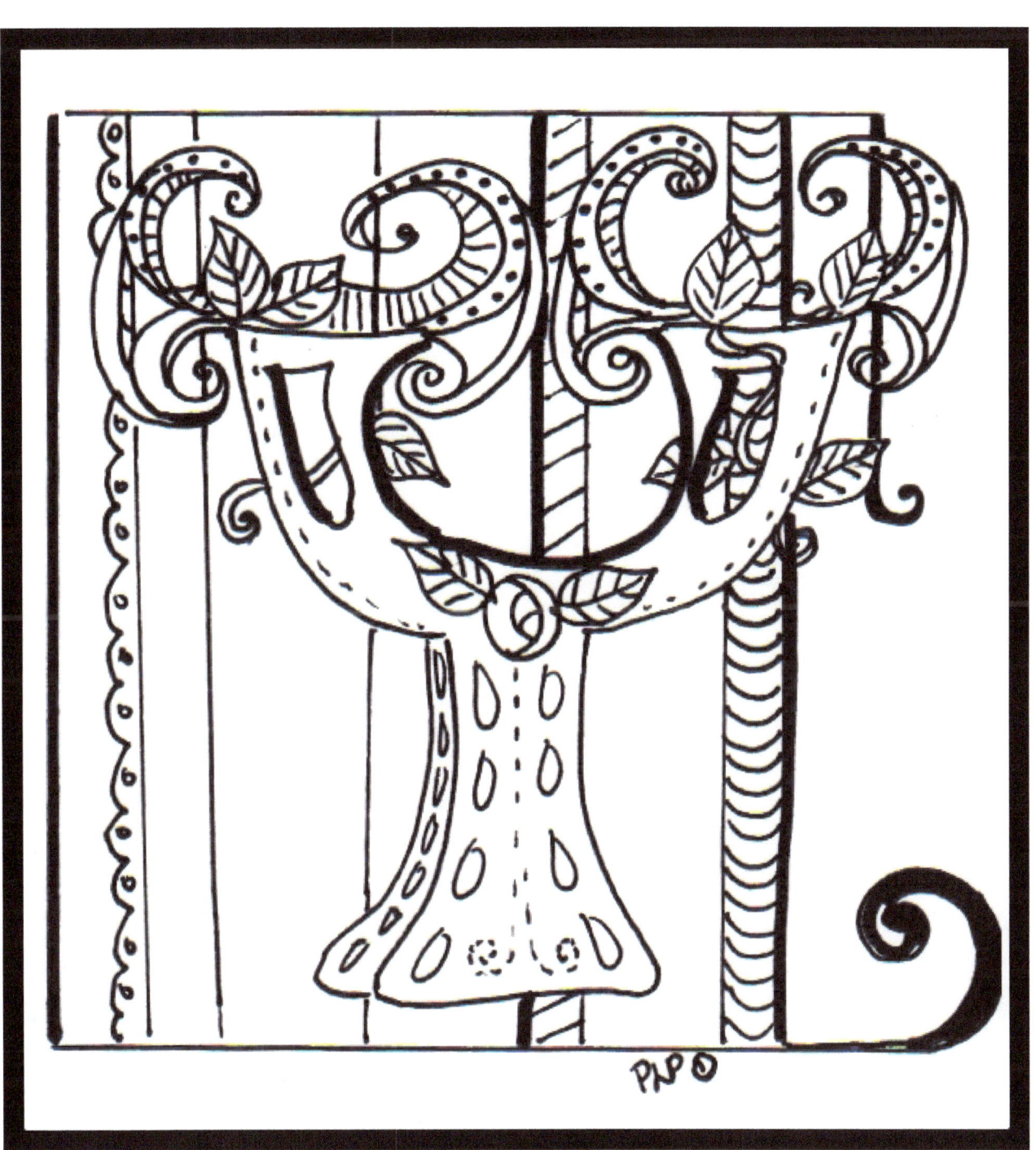

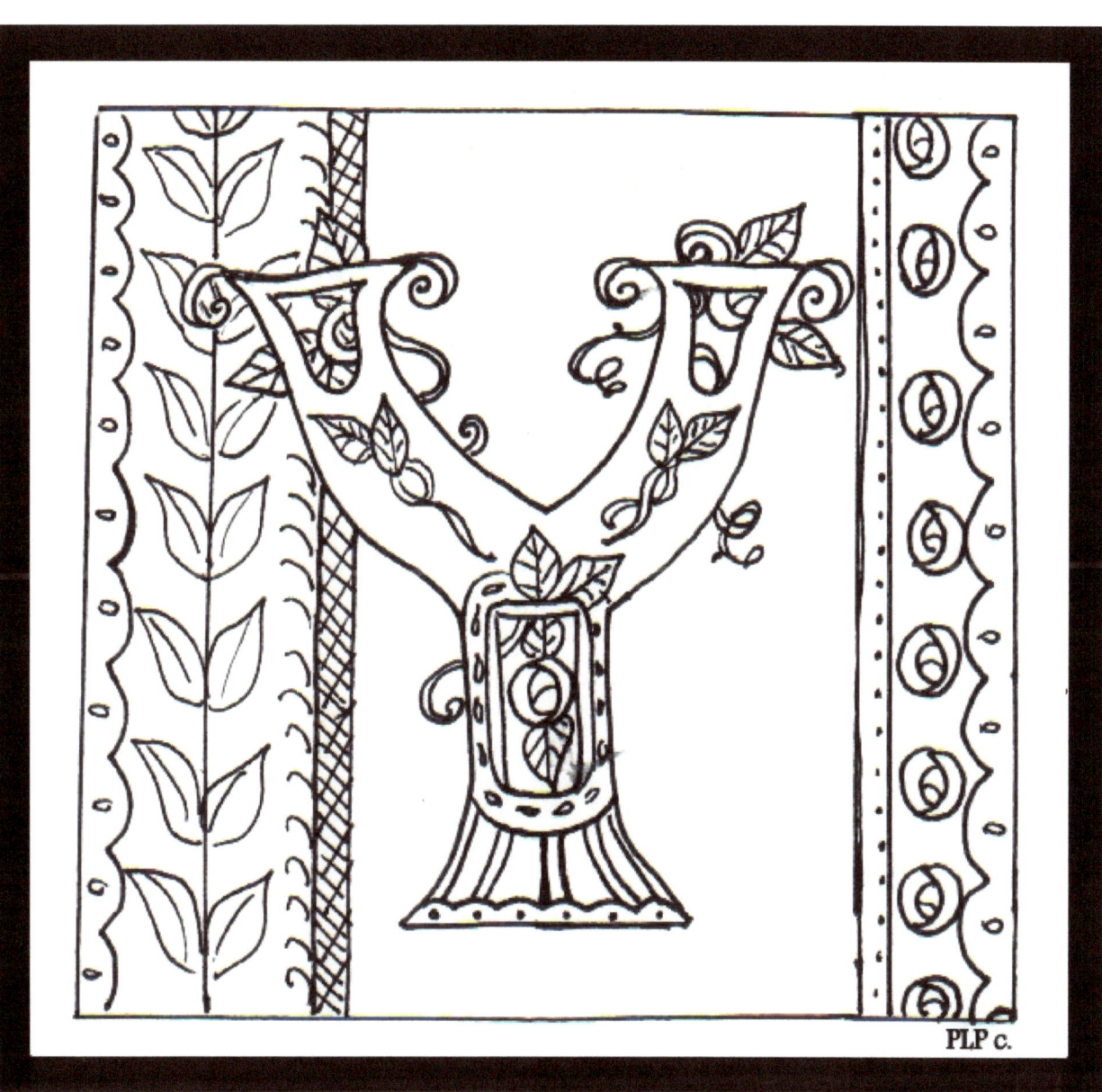

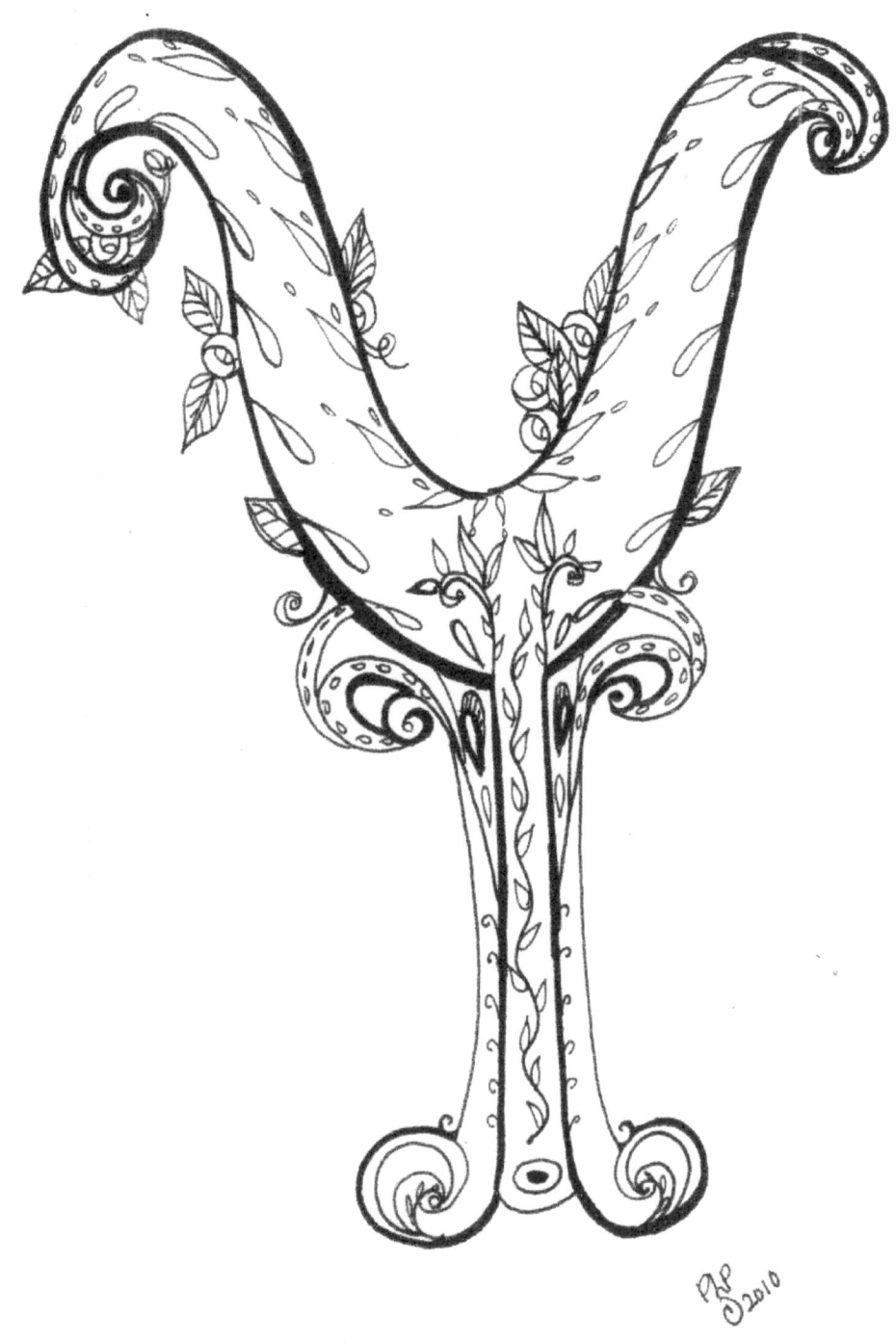

43

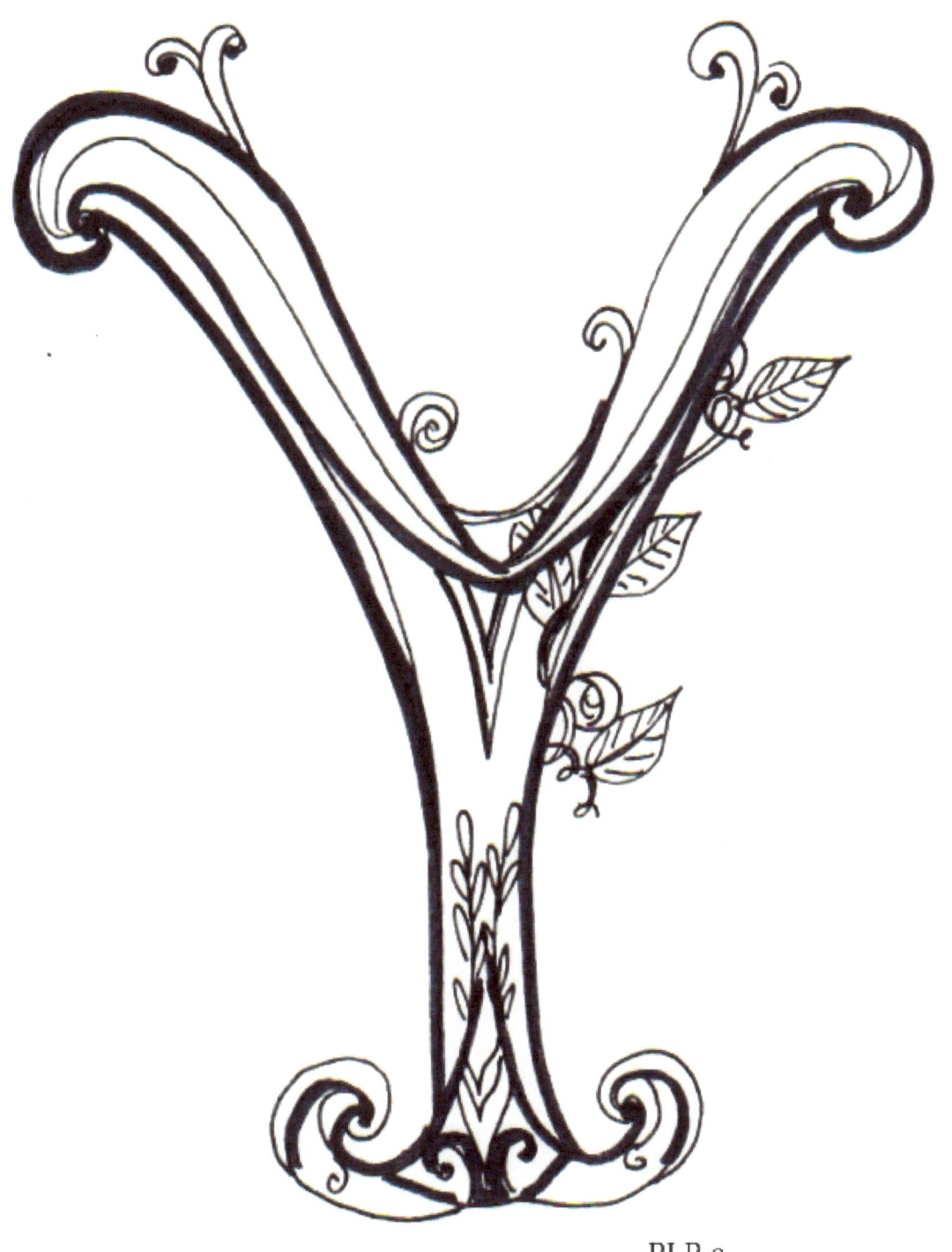

PLP c.

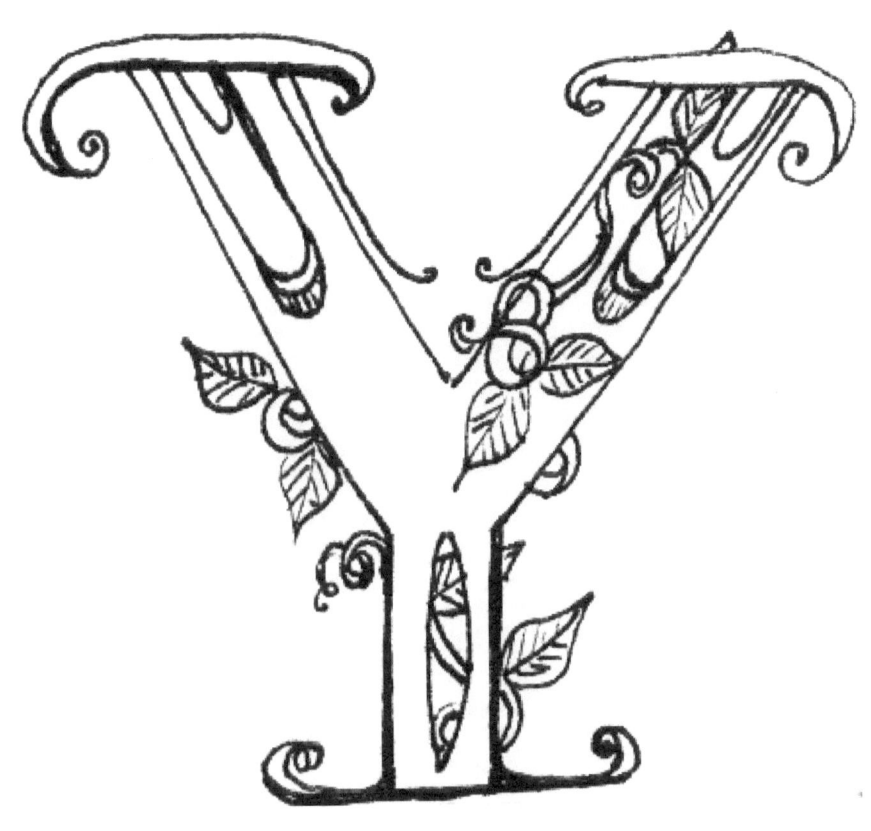

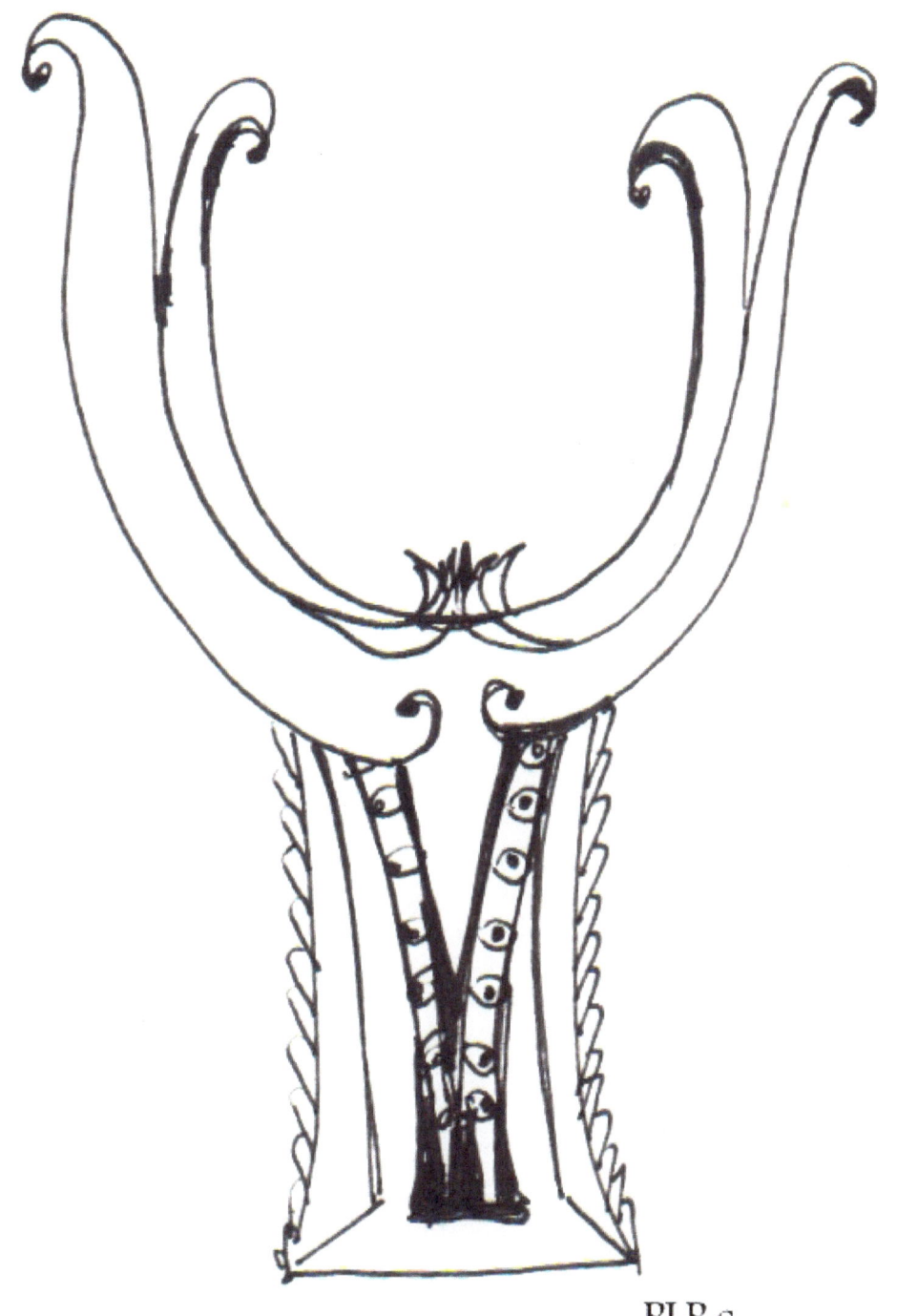

PLP c.

51

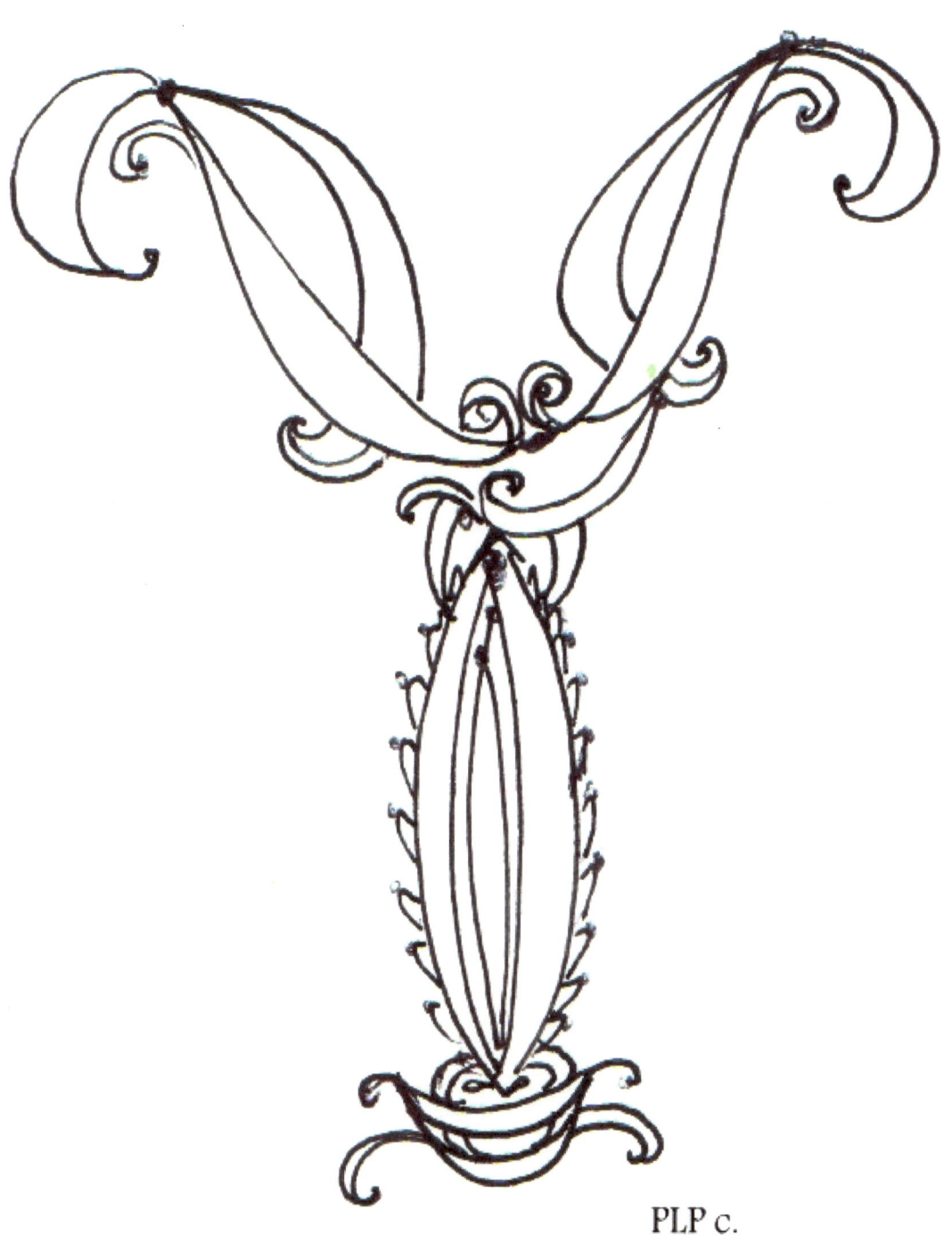

PLP c.

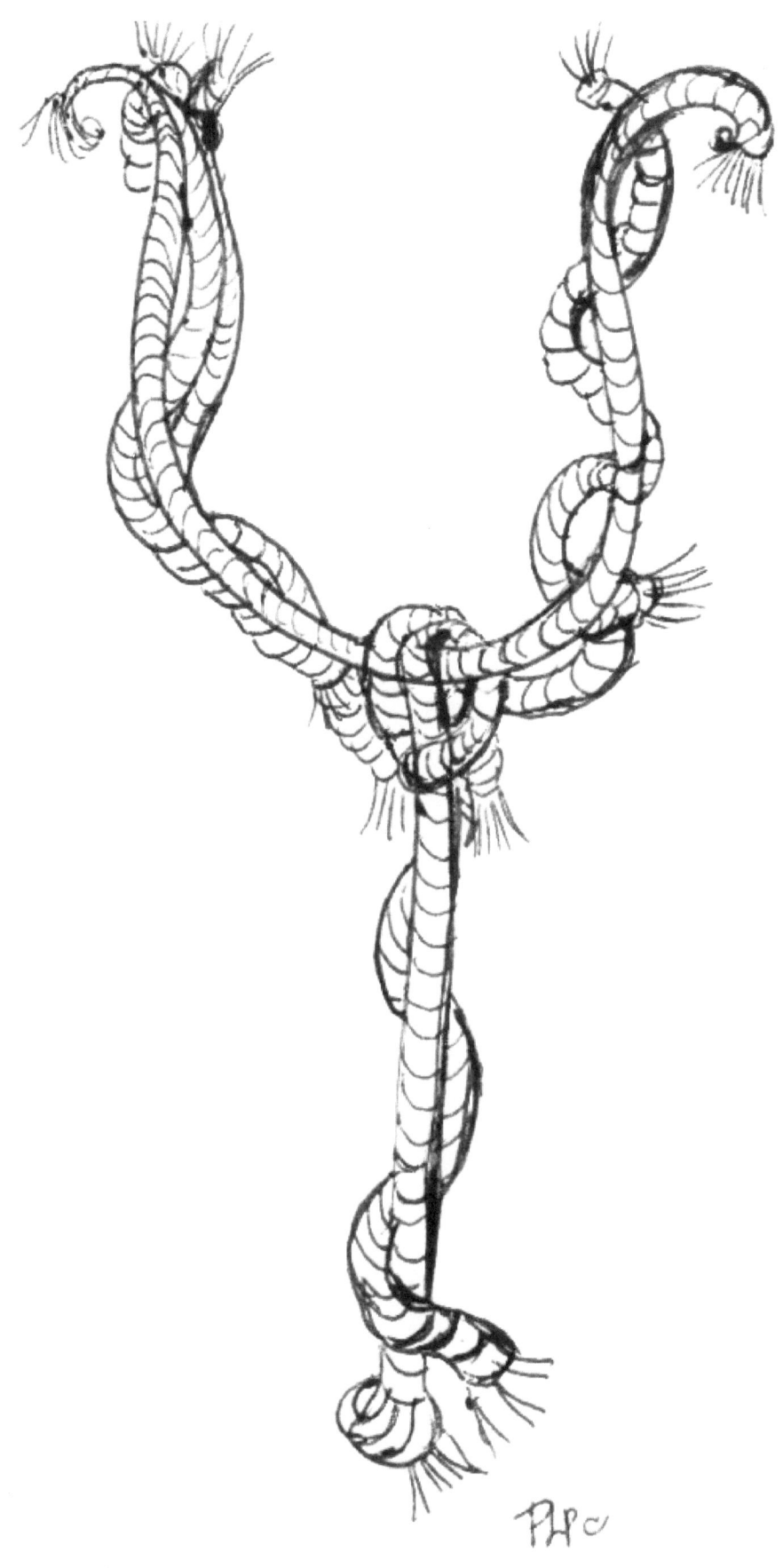

55

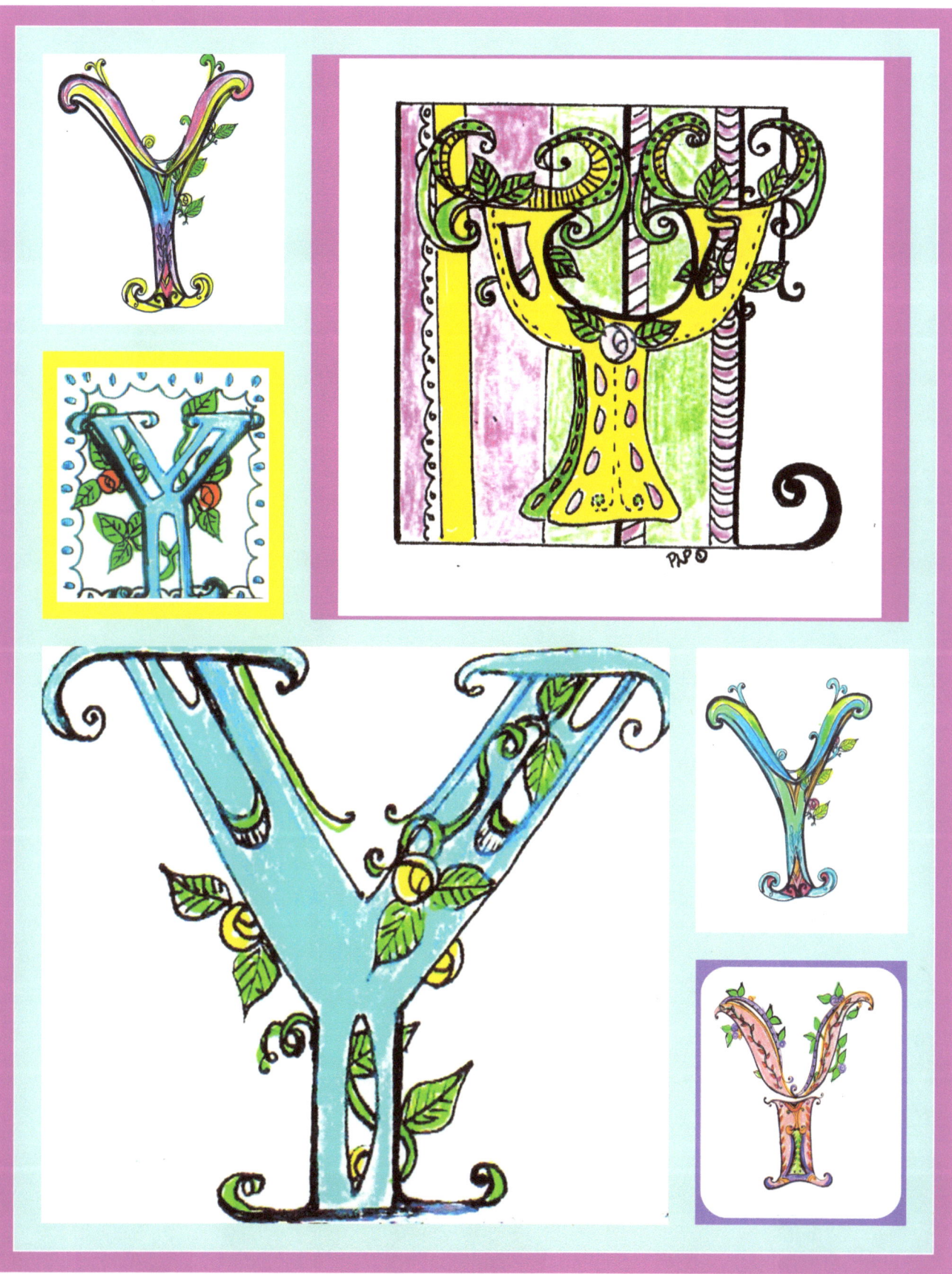

I hope YOUR adventure with letter Y gives you smiles and

many new ideas for the letter Y's in your world.

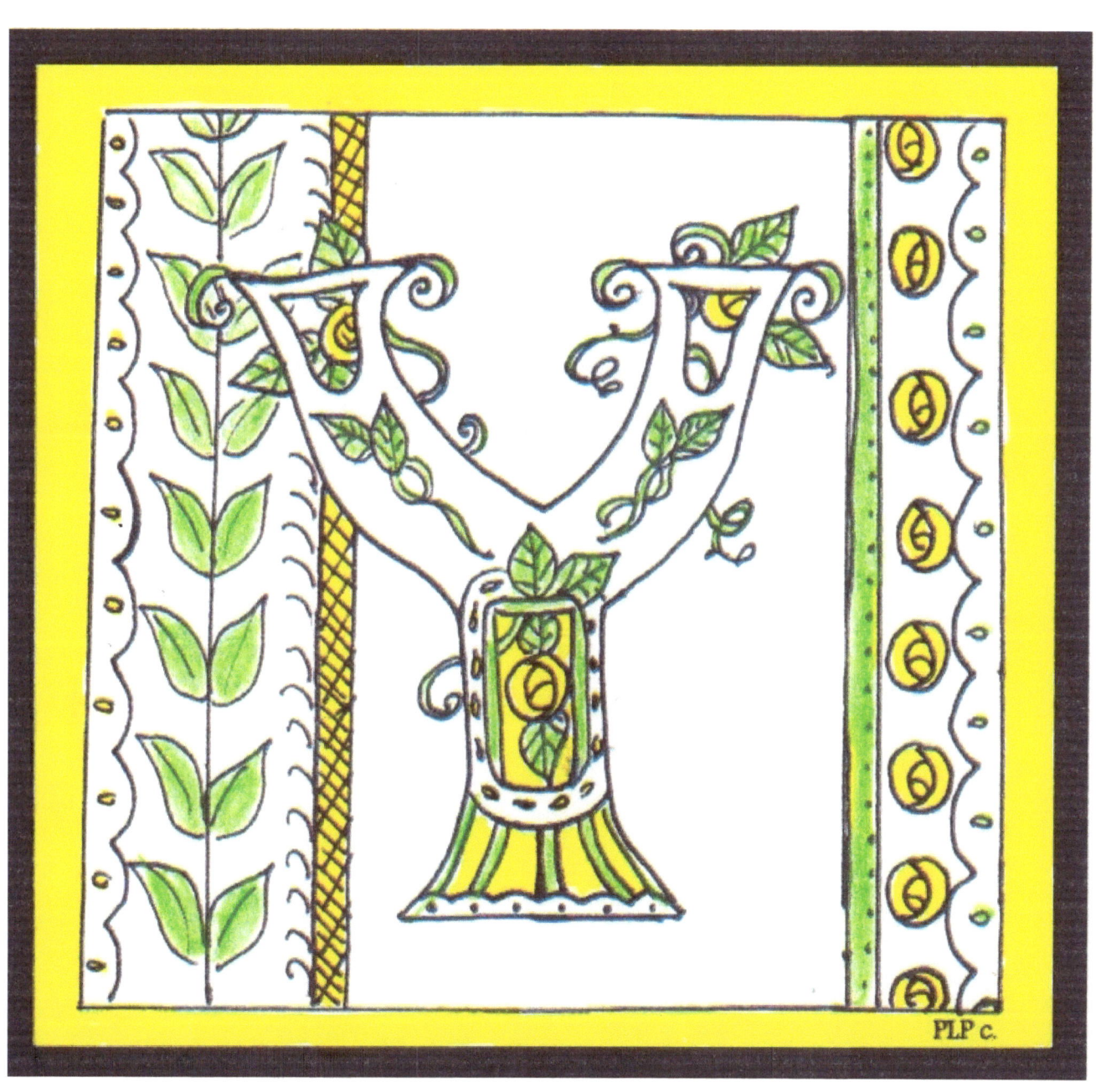